The Spiritual Sync

SJ Baldridge

Published by SJ Baldridge, 2021.

While every precaution has been taken in the preparation of this book, the publisher assumes no responsibility for errors or omissions, or for damages resulting from the use of the information contained herein.

THE SPIRITUAL SYNC

First edition. October 2, 2021.

ISBN: 979-8201723194

Written by SJ Baldridge.

Table of Contents

"It is necessary for him to increase and for me to decrease." John 3:30 The Passion Translation

The Spiritual Sync: 21 Days of Syncing with the Spirit

In sync. Bands and soldiers march in sync. We are mesmerized by lip sync contests. Companies and families need to work in sync with each other. We all know how important it is to sync our technology, and some of us may have even suffered the consequences of not syncing our technological devices.

Being in sync in this fast-paced, modern world is crucial, and yet, the key to actually being—and living—in sync is not what one would expect.

The key to being in sync with our technology is to stop, connect, and allow time for our devices to sync.

The key to being in sync with our spiritual life is no different; we need to stop, connect, and allow time to sync with our Maker. To sync our spirit with God's Holy Spirit.

Thus, The Spiritual Sync! Let us be purposeful and spend the next 21 days—syncing with the Spirit. We will do that in three easy steps—well, actually, you will determine the degree of difficulty and the schedule for yourselves. My intent for us was to create new routines and habits by setting aside time during each of the next 21 days. If possible, make every effort to stick with the daily plan, but we all understand how life works sometimes. Do what works for you knowing that God does bless us when we make time for Him in our lives.

Step One: Set aside time to listen to the Holy Spirit. *(Please start with a minimum of 10 minutes just sitting quietly before the Lord. Hey, we know it takes our phones more than 10 minutes to recharge; why would we be any different?) If it helps, journal thoughts during this time; this can also end up being a powerful record of the Holy Spirit's work in our lives during our Spiritual Sync.*

Step Two: Read verses and accounts from Scripture that show the Holy Spirit's work. In each of our 21 days, we will explore the Spirit at work throughout the Old and the New Testaments.

Step Three: Pray, reflect, and watch for the Spirit's work in our own lives. *If we don't actually ask, expect, and watch for the work of the Holy Spirit in our lives, how can we even know whether we are in sync with what God has in store for us?*

As a mom who has raised four children, I know how hectic days can be as we maneuver through the complicated maze of our family's schedules. *Let's sync our spirit with God's Spirit during these next 21 days. Let's quiet our bodies, our minds, and our hearts, and sync up with what God truly wants to say to us through the Holy Spirit.*

I am excited that you have chosen to join this exciting Spiritual Sync!

Day #1 Who is the Spirit?

The Holy Spirit. The Spirit of God. The Breath of the Almighty. The Counselor and Comforter. The Spirit of Understanding. These are just a few of the names or titles attributed to the Holy Spirit in Scripture. Beyond these titles, who is the Spirit and why is it important for us to be in sync with the Holy Spirit?

Today let's begin our routine.

Step One: Spend 10 minutes quieting your world and your heart before we continue. Let's trust in a favorite verse from Psalm 46:10, "Be still and know that I am God." (So, let's make our world as quiet as possible. I'm serious; it is extremely difficult to hear from the Spirit while scrolling social media or with an episode of *Friends* in the background.) *It works for me to try to quiet my heart first; if it works better for you to read the Scriptures and then have quiet time, do whatever works best for you.*

Step Two: Scripture

Our verses today center upon "In the beginning..."

We know this familiar phrase from Genesis, but we often overlook the Holy Spirit in verse 2. The Holy Spirit was there at Creation. **Proverbs 8** is a chapter about Wisdom. The verses explain how Wisdom (the Holy Spirit) was present at Creation. If possible, read all of Proverbs 8; you won't regret it.

Genesis 1:2 states, "*Now the earth was formless and empty, darkness was over the surface of the deep, and the Spirit of God was hovering over the waters.*"

Proverbs 8:22-23

"*The Lord brought me forth as the first of his works, before his deeds of old; I was formed long ages ago, at the very beginning, when the world came to be.*"

Proverbs 8:32-35 offers advice from the Holy Spirit to each of us:

"*Now then, my children, listen to me; blessed are those who keep my ways. Listen to my instruction and be wise; do not disregard it. Blessed are those who listen to me, watching daily at my doors, waiting at my doorway. For those who find me find life and receive favor from the Lord.*"

Step Three: Pray, reflect, and watch for the Spirit's work in our own lives. What is the Holy Spirit of God saying to us today? Many of us are familiar with **Jeremiah 29:11**, in which God declares that He has a plan for us, and it is a plan that prospers us. *Isn't it in our best interest to surrender to God's plan for us?—for us to be in sync with our Maker?*

Prayer: Almighty God, We thank You for Your Holy Word. We thank You for the Holy Spirit who guides us each day. We surrender to You and to Your Plan for our lives. We desire to grow closer to You, Lord, and to sync our lives with Your Will. In Jesus' Name. Amen

"*Since we live by the Spirit, let us keep in step with the Spirit.*" *~Galatians 5:25*

Day #2 Ruach Elohim

Welcome! It's day #2, and we are going to dive in to look at some Hebrew, the language of the Old Testament.

Ruach: Hebrew word meaning breath, wind, spirit

When *ruach* is paired with a name for God, it refers to the Holy Spirit. ***Ruach Elohim*** is what is written in Genesis 1:2 from yesterday.

Isn't that beautiful? God is truly breath, wind, and spirit as we will see throughout our time together.

Why do we need to sync with the Holy Spirit?

As I was sitting on my deck this morning (before the rain), I was watching the birds. A bird's wings work in unison to fly. With those two little wings working together, the bird can soar to the tops of the trees. Now, we have our own spirit (that would be one wing), and as a Christian we have the Holy Spirit (the other wing); if we do not work with the Holy Spirit, our spirit will never soar as God intended.

Let's go through our routine.

Step One: First, let's relax. Breathe. Let's be intentional about giving God the next 10 minutes. Let's quiet our hearts and minds before we continue.

***Psalm 46:10a** *"He [God] says, 'Be still, and know that I am God...'"*

As we quiet our bodies, hearts, and minds from our worldly concerns, we might focus on **Proverbs 8:30**, in which we can visualize the Holy Spirit's involvement at Creation: *"Then I was beside Him as a master craftsman; And I was daily His delight, Rejoicing always before Him,"* (NKJV). The ESV states, *"then I was beside him, like a master workman, and I was daily his delight, rejoicing before him always."*

Step Two: Scripture

Today in Scripture we are going to look at two beautiful promises. One in the Old Testament, and one in the New.

Ezekiel 36:26-27

"I will give you a new heart and put a new spirit in you: I will remove from you your heart of stone and give you a heart of flesh. And I will put my Spirit in you and move you to follow my decrees and be careful to keep my laws."

God is showing both understanding and love here. He knows that we have been beaten up by this world, and that numerous experiences have toughened and hardened our hearts. God will not only give us a heart of flesh, but He even goes further in the next verse when He promises to put His Spirit (*Ruach Elohim*) in us to guide us. Oh, our loving God!

2 Timothy 1:7

"For the Spirit God gave us does not make us timid, but gives us power, love and self-discipline." NIV

"For God has not given us a spirit of fear and timidity, but of power, love, and self-discipline." NLT

How encouraging! God has given us the Holy Spirit. That Holy Spirit has Almighty power (was part of Creation), and that Spirit lives within us to work on our hearts and to guide us through this life.

Step Three: Pray, reflect, and watch for the Spirit's work in our own lives. What is the Holy Spirit of God saying to us today?

God knows us and wants good for us. When we acknowledge Jesus Christ as our Lord and Savior, God gives us His Holy Spirit to guide us, and when our spirit is in sync with *Ruach Elohim (God's Spirit),* we can soar!

Prayer: Almighty God, You are the Creator and Everlasting God. We acknowledge Jesus as our Savior and Redeemer. Thank you for Your promises in Scripture and the gift of Your Spirit. Forgive us our disobedience and help us to learn to live in sync with the Holy Spirit. Help us to recognize Your work in our lives today. In Jesus' Name. Amen.

"Since we live by the Spirit, let us keep in step with the Spirit." ~Galatians 5:25

Day #3 The Room Where It Happens

Be alone with God? Listen for the Holy Spirit to speak? Where do I go to experience this wonder? I want to meet and talk with God, but much like in one of the famous songs from the musical *Hamilton,* I feel like I am never in "The Room Where It Happens."

Fortunately, we don't actually need to change rooms; we just need to change our mindsets. God is so gracious; He is willing to meet us. Wherever we choose to quiet our hearts and listen and communicate with God Almighty is "The Room Where It Happens."

Today let's go through our routine.

Step One: Spend 10 minutes quieting our world and our hearts before we continue. Playing calming music can help with this. I choose to ask Alexa to play "light Classical" music; I believe she then pulls up a list entitled "Classical Focus." I begin with a deep breath, and I ask the Spirit to guide my thoughts over the next ten minutes.

Step Two: Scripture

Psalm 104 This entire chapter is beautiful and paints quite a picture of God's power in Creation. We are going to focus on just two verses, but if possible, read all of Psalm 104.

Psalm 104:30 This verse reminds us again of the Holy Spirit's work during Creation as the breath of life.

"When you send your Spirit, they are created, and you renew the face of the ground."

Psalm 104:34 (This is a verse that can guide our 10 minutes of reflection each day.)

"May my meditation be pleasing to him, as I rejoice in the Lord."

Isaiah 30:21 (and **19-20**) ****_This verse is so worth memorizing._** It is a verse I memorized years ago, and these words have guided me through numerous challenges. Just this week the Holy Spirit guided me to also focus on the two verses before it, so let's look at all three.

"People of Zion, who live in Jerusalem, you will weep no more. How gracious he will be when you cry for help! As soon as he hears, he will answer you. Although the Lord gives you the bread of adversity and the water of affliction, your teachers will be hidden no more; with your own eyes you will see them. Whether you turn to the right or to the left, your ears will hear a voice behind you, saying, 'This is the way; walk in it.'"

Step Three: Pray, reflect, and watch for the Spirit's work in our own lives. What is the Holy Spirit of God saying to us today? Wherever we pray is *the room where it happens.* Much like the famed "Situation Room" in Washington D.C., God wants to guide us in His great plans for us, and as we walk along, God's Word promises that He will direct us with the Spirit's voice.

Prayer: Almighty God, We thank You for Your Holy Word. We thank you that You meet us and offer guidance to us. We thank You for the voice that guides us as we walk each day with You, Lord. Help

our meditation be pleasing to You, Almighty God, as we rejoice in You. In Jesus' Name. Amen.

"Since we live by the Spirit, let us keep in step with the Spirit." ~Galatians 5:25

A Prayer Process:

When I was a young Christian, one of my insecurities was prayer. I was sure that there was a "right" way, and that I hadn't learned the secret yet. So, as with any relationship, communication is key, and yet, I felt insecure about communicating with God because I felt like I didn't know how.

The following verses freed me from my feelings of insecurity.

Nehemiah 2:1-5a

"In the month of Nisan in the twentieth year of King Artaxerxes, when wine was brought for him, I took the wine and gave it to the king. I had not been sad in his presence before, so the king asked me, 'Why does your face look so sad when you are not ill? This can be nothing but sadness of heart.'

I was very much afraid, but I said to the king, 'May the king live forever! Why should my face not look sad when the city where my ancestors are buried lies in ruins, and its gates have been destroyed by fire?'

The king said to me, 'What is it you want?'

Then I prayed to the God of heaven, and I answered the king,..."

We have to pay attention to the order of events in the scene. Nehemiah—cupbearer to the king—was sad. When Nehemiah explained the problem to the king, the king asked Nehemiah, "What is it you want?"

What happens next?

Nehemiah prays to the God of heaven. He prays.

Standing in the presence of the king of the land, Nehemiah pauses to pray to the King of Kings.

I Thessalonians 5:17

"pray continually,"

Matthew 6 includes Jesus' own advice to us about prayer:

Matthew 6:6-7a, 9-13

"But when you pray, go into your room, close the door and pray to your Father, who is unseen. Then your Father, who sees what is done in secret, will

reward you. And when you pray, do not keep on babbling like pagans...This, then, is how you should pray:

> *'Our Father in heaven,*
> *Hallowed be your name,*
> *Your kingdom come, your will be done,*
> *On earth as it is in heaven.*
> *Give us today our daily bread.*
> *And forgive us our debts, as we also have forgiven our debtors.*
> *And lead us not into temptation, but deliver us from the evil one....'"*

How can we grow more secure in our relationship with God? How can we be more confident with our prayers?

Take time to meet with God. Take time to pray to God. Take time to read God's Word.

Something that helped me these past few months is to add a few actions in order to focus my attention as I pray.

The following is a little bit of a "guided visualization" that may enhance our time with Almighty God.

Guided Visualization for Quiet Time

Sit tall, close your eyes, and take a deep breath in through your nose.

Completely fill your lungs and hold for a count of four.

Let the breath empty slowly through your mouth.

Hold your right hand out in front of you, palm up.—Think to yourself that this right hand connects to your personal thoughts, and your personal will.

Go ahead and allow thoughts, concerns, and plans for the day to fill your minds, and visualize setting each of these ideas in the palm of your right hand.

Let these thoughts rest there. Make a fist in order to gather up all of these thoughts.

Take another deep breath in through your nose.

Completely fill your lungs and hold for a count of four. Release the breath slowly through your mouth.

Hold your left hand out in front of you, palm up.—Think to yourself that this left hand connects to your heart, (and the Holy Spirit).

Think and say the words, "God's Will."

Move your right fist to rest on your left hand.

Take another deep breath.

Slowly, open your right fist in order to release all of your own thoughts, concerns, and plans for the day onto your left hand (God's Will).

Speak any of the following words as you picture yourself releasing hold of all of those concerns and letting them rest in God's Will.

"I surrender all."

"Not my will, but thine be done, Lord God."

"Holy Spirit, guide me this day."

"Lord, you are the One and only God. I release this day's worries, cares, and concerns into Your Good and Capable Hands. In Jesus' Name. Amen"

Now, lift your right hand away from the left knowing and trusting (having faith) that God will guide you in the path you should go today.

Enjoy this promise from God's Word. **Isaiah 41:13**

"For I am the LORD your God who takes hold of your right hand and says to you, Do not fear; I will help you."

Take one more deep breath as you picture the scene that this verse creates.

We know that God is there, and that Jesus is at God's right hand.—But this verse adds *you* into the picture. *"...I am the LORD your God who takes hold of your right hand..."*

Oh, what a beautiful scene! You see, quiet time with the Lord is worth it and will help us cast away our earthly cares. The song "Turn Your Eyes upon Jesus" comes to my mind after all of this:

"Turn your eyes upon Jesus

Look full, in his wonderful face

And the things of earth will grow strangely dim

In the light of his glory and grace."

Caution/Disclaimer

Prayer is *not* a promise that everything will go beautifully today and that we will have no cares.

This *is* a promise that God will be with us through everything, and also that whatever we face today will lead us to the privilege of glorifying God.

John 16:33

[Jesus said] *"I have told you these things, so that in me you may have peace. In this world you will have trouble. But take heart! I have overcome the world."*

I truly hope and pray that each of us pray continually, trusting God with our daily concerns.

Day #4 Hoarders Beware!

The camera pans on the scene of a home where a person is surrounded by baskets, newspapers, puzzles, clothing, fast food cartons, Christmas decorations, *Star Wars* memorabilia, etc. This person has little room to move about with belongings piled up in every direction. We want to look away, and yet we are strangely riveted by the scene. We're curious; how did this person get into this situation, and is there any chance of making a change?

We can clutter our hearts in the same way individuals on *Hoarders* clutter their worlds. Today we are going to face the clutter that we have been hoarding and clean out our hearts. It's time.

Spiritual Sync routine:

Step One: Spend 10 minutes quieting our world and our hearts before we continue. Take a deep breath, acknowledge God as Lord and Savior, and ask the Spirit to help us "Be still and know God." We might also ask the Holy Spirit to reveal to us those things that are cluttering our hearts. We might try the Prayer Process from Day #3.

Step Two: Scripture

David is referred to in Scripture as "a man after God's own heart." David famously fought Goliath with a slingshot and stones, he ruled Israel, and he was a mighty warrior for the Lord. He also had a passionate relationship with the Lord which is seen in the numerous Psalms written by him. We are going to look at the selection and anointing of David; this is also the moment David was filled with the Spirit. We are also going to look at a portion of the heartbreaking Psalm in which David asks forgiveness of God.

I Samuel 16:7

"But the Lord said to Samuel, 'Do not consider his appearance or his height, for I have rejected him. The Lord does not look at the things people look at. People look at the outward appearance, but the Lord looks at the heart."

I Samuel 16:13

"So Samuel took the horn of oil and anointed him in the presence of his brothers, and from that day on the Spirit of the Lord came powerfully upon David..."

Psalm 51:10-12

"Create in me a pure heart, O God, and renew a steadfast spirit within me.

Do not cast me from your presence or take your Holy Spirit from me.

Restore to me the joy of your salvation and grant me a willing spirit, to sustain me."

Step Three: Pray, reflect, and watch for the Spirit's work in our own lives. What is the Holy Spirit of God saying to us today?

The Spirit is telling me to stop cluttering my heart with my sin, my guilt, and my shame. I don't need all the distractions of the world. I need to submit to God; I need to ask the Holy Spirit to "create in me a pure heart." What is the Holy Spirit saying to you?

Hopefully, as we continue this Spiritual Sync, we will have the same sentiments towards God as David did in **Psalm 63:1-4.**

"You, God, are my God, earnestly I seek you; I thirst for you, my whole being longs for you, in a dry and parched land where there is no water.

I have seen you in the sanctuary and beheld your power and your glory.

Because your love is better than life, my lips will glorify you.

I will praise you as long as I live, and in your name I will lift up my hands."

Prayer: Gracious God, thank you for Your merciful kindness. Lord, forgive us for the sin, guilt, and shame we have cluttered and stored in our hearts. Help us to accept Your forgiveness and mercy, and help us to now seek You with all our hearts. In Jesus' Name. Amen.

"Since we live by the Spirit, let us keep in step with the Spirit." ~Galatians 5:25

Day #5 Limitless Power/Quiet Voice

Have you ever had the experience of getting to know someone's voice, and then meeting that person and then having a conflict within yourself because the person behind the voice wasn't who/what you had expected? Today during our time we are going to go through just this struggle. We are going to look at verses that proclaim the strength and power of God's Spirit, and yet we are also going to read about a time when Elijah not only experienced God's still, small voice, but also God's great, mighty power.

Spiritual Sync routine:

Step One: Spend 10 minutes quieting our world and our hearts before we continue. Take a deep breath, acknowledge God as Lord and Savior, and ask the Spirit to help us "Be still and know God." We might also ask the Holy Spirit to allow us to discern God's voice from all the other noises in our world.

Step Two: Scripture *Let's look at more of the work of the God's Spirit in the Old Testament.*

Joseph was able to interpret the Pharaoh's dream through the work of the Holy Spirit, and as a result, even Pharaoh recognized the power of the Lord God.

Genesis 41:38-40

"So Pharaoh asked them, 'Can we find anyone like this man, one in whom is the spirit of God?" Then Pharaoh said to Joseph, 'Since God has made all this known to you, there is no one so discerning and wise as you. You shall be in charge of my palace, and all my people are to submit to your orders. Only with respect to the throne will I be greater than you.'"

Moses & 70 Elders: **Numbers 11:25** reveals that not only was the Spirit of God within Moses, but that the power of that Spirit was shared among 70 elders within the community. *"Then the LORD came down in the cloud and spoke with him, and he took some of the power of the Spirit that was on him and put it on the seventy elders. When the Spirit rested on them, they prophesied—but did not do so again."*

Gideon: In **Judges 6:34a** we read about the Spirit of the Lord coming upon Gideon.

Samson: Judges reveals numerous times that the "Spirit of the Lord came powerfully" upon Samson.

These are just a few of the times in God's Word in which the power of the Holy Spirit is revealed. Powerful God, Powerful Voice, right? Now, let's read about a time when Elijah was filled with doubt, even after witnessing the power of God's Spirit in his own life on numerous occasions. Elijah is actually desperate in this portion of **I Kings 19:11-12.**

"The LORD said, 'Go out and stand on the mountain in the presence of the LORD, for the LORD is about to pass by.'

Then a great and powerful wind tore the mountains apart and shattered the rocks before the LORD, but the LORD was not in the wind. After the wind there was an earthquake, but the LORD was not in the earthquake. After the earthquake came a fire, but the LORD was not in the fire. And after the fire came a gentle whisper. When Elijah heard it, he pulled his cloak over his face and went out and stood at the mouth of the cave.

Then a voice said to him, 'What are you doing here, Elijah?'"

Ahh, the whisper. The gentle whisper is where the Lord could be found.

Step Three: Pray, reflect, and watch for the Spirit's work in our own lives. What is the Holy Spirit of God saying to us today?

Today, let us be bold and ask two things of the Lord: Open our eyes to the powerful works of the Spirit and open our ears to hear the gentle whisper of the Holy Spirit saying, "this is the way, walk in it." ***Isaiah 50:4b,*** *"He [God] wakens me morning by morning, wakens my ear to listen like one being instructed."*

Prayer: Almighty God, we want to know you. Please help us to submit to the Spirit within us. We ask that You open our eyes to the powerful works of the Holy Spirit that are all around us, and open our ears, Lord, to hear Your still, small voice. In Jesus' Name. Amen.

"Since we live by the Spirit, let us keep in step with the Spirit." ~Galatians 5:25

Day #6 My Confession

I need to confess. I wasn't clear at the start. I haven't been planning this Spiritual Sync for weeks and months. This is something that the Holy Spirit put on my heart because *I needed this*. I needed to sync up with the Spirit, and I wanted to allow others to come along in this journey.

Another confession. I can be easily distracted at times—okay, honestly, I can be easily distracted *a lot* of the time. I have good intentions, but my attention can float much like a butterfly flitting from flower to flower through a vibrant garden.

Fortunately, the Holy Spirit is able to help each of us in numerous ways.

Spiritual Sync routine:

Step One: Spend 10 minutes quieting our world and our hearts before we continue. Take a deep breath, acknowledge God as Lord and Savior, and confess that we need help with getting in sync with the Lord.

Step Two: Today we are going to look at a few of my favorite verses. This may even lead to us challenging ourselves to find a few of our favorite verses and committing these verses to memory.

Micah 6:8 These are wonderful words to live by each day.

"He has shown you, O mortal, what is good. And what does the Lord require of you?

To act justly and to love mercy and to walk humbly with your God."

Philippians 3:12-14 The short version of these words is the familiar expression: "Be patient, God isn't finished with me yet."

"Not that I have already obtained all this, or have already arrived at my goal, but I press on to take hold of that for which Christ Jesus took hold of me. Brothers and sisters, I do not consider myself yet to have taken hold of it. But one thing I do: Forgetting what is behind and straining toward what is ahead, I press on toward the goal to win the prize for which God has called me heavenward in Christ Jesus."

2 Corinthians 10:5b Words to help us focus.

"...and we take captive every thought to make it obedient to Christ."

Psalm 143:8-10

"Let the morning bring me word of your unfailing love,

for I have put my trust in you.

Show me the way I should go, for to you I entrust my life.

Rescue me from my enemies, Lord, for I hide myself in you.

Teach me to do your will, for you are my God;

may your good Spirit lead me on level ground."

Step Three: Pray, reflect, and watch for the Spirit's work in our own lives. What is the Holy Spirit of God saying to us today?

Maybe you have a confession of your own to share with God. If so, have quiet time to ask for the Holy Spirit's guidance with this confession.

I know I need to ask for my own assistance as I strive to keep my focus on growing closer with the Lord.

Prayer: Almighty God, we confess that we need the Spirit's guidance in order to help us know you better. We can let so many things in this world distract us. Show us the way, Lord, and help us take captive our thoughts. In Jesus' Name. Amen.

"Since we live by the Spirit, let us keep in step with the Spirit." ~Galatians 5:25

Day #7 Holy Power

I hope the power of this Spiritual Sync is beginning to "sink" in (not even trying to be punny). We began one week ago, and our goal is to get "in sync" with the Holy Spirit of God over our 21 days together. We know the Holy Spirit is the breath of the Almighty and was involved in Creation. We also know that the same Spirit, with all of that Holy Power, is at work in our lives and has promised to give us a new heart of flesh. We just need to remain in sync with the Spirit.

Tomorrow, we will begin week #2 of this 3-week journey, and we will look at the Holy Spirit and Jesus, but for today, let's explore a few more passages from the Old Testament. These passages reveal the Holy Spirit at work in the correcting of God's people, in the building of the temple, and in revealing prophecy.

As we explore these, take a moment to consider how much more access we have to the Lord God today as opposed to during Old Testament times. Many of us have the Bible app on our phones and can access any verse at any time (in numerous translations). Let's not take these precious words for granted.

Spiritual Sync routine:

Step One: Spend 10 minutes quieting our world and our hearts before we continue. Take captive every thought.

Step Two: Scripture *Let's look at more of the work of God's Spirit in the Old Testament.*

Isaiah 44:3

"For I will pour water on the thirsty land, and streams on the dry ground;

I will pour out my Spirit on your offspring, and my blessing on your descendants."

Ezekiel 37:1-10 The Holy Spirit actually makes the dry bones move and come to life.

"The hand of the Lord was on me, and he brought me out by the Spirit of the Lord and set me in the middle of a valley; it was full of bones. He led me back and forth among them, and I saw a great many bones on the floor of the valley, bones that were very dry. He asked me, 'Son of man, can these bones live?'

I said, 'Sovereign Lord, you alone know.'

Then he said to me, 'Prophesy to these bones and say to them, 'Dry bones, hear the word of the Lord! This is what the Sovereign Lord says to these bones: I will make breath enter you, and you will come to life. I will attach tendons to you and make flesh come upon you and cover you with skin; I will put breath in you, and you will come to life. Then you will know that I am the Lord.'

So I prophesied as I was commanded. And as I was prophesying, there was a noise, a rattling sound, and the bones came together, bone to bone. I looked, and tendons and flesh appeared on them and skin covered them, but there was no breath in them.

Then he said to me, 'Prophesy to the breath; prophesy, son of man, and say to it, 'This is what the Sovereign Lord says: Come, breath, from the four winds and breathe into these slain, that they may live.' So I prophesied as he commanded me, and breath entered them; they came to life and stood up on their feet—a vast army."

Micah 3:8a

"But as for me, I am filled with power, with the Spirit of the Lord, and with justice and might..."

Exodus 31:1-5 (and repeated in **Exodus 35:31-33**)

"The Lord said to Moses, 'See, I have chosen Bezalel...and I have filled him with the Spirit of God, with wisdom, with understanding, with knowledge and with all kinds of skills—to make artistic designs for work in gold, silver and bronze, to cut and set stones, to work in wood, and to engage in all kinds of crafts."

**Isn't this magnificent? The Holy Spirit of God can bring bones to life and yet also provides creative and artistic talents. The point of these selections is to show the limitless power and range of God's Spirit. The Spirit gives wisdom, predicts the future, doles out God's justice, and even, gives artistic talents for the creation of the Tabernacle.

Step Three: Pray, reflect, and watch for the Spirit's work in our own lives. What is the Holy Spirit of God saying to us today?

Lord God, You are full of power and goodness. We are thankful for the Holy Spirit at work in our lives. God, guide us in reading and learning more about You and Your Holy Spirit. We truly want to live in step with Your plan for our lives. In the Name of Jesus Christ. Amen.

"Since we live by the Spirit, let us keep in step with the Spirit." ~Galatians 5:25

Day #8 He? She? It?

Okay, so of course, the Holy Spirit is part of the Trinity, and certainly, the Holy Spirit is powerful, but since our world is striving for more accurate pronouns and labels, which should be used for the Holy Spirit?

While I have explored this topic quite a bit, I am going to begin at the end—with my conclusion. I will then back up and give my rationale, and let you decide. First, I need to be clear that I am not talking in terms of the Battle of the Sexes—male vs. female war that seems to be pushed by society and the media. This isn't about better or power, because God is God. God is omnipotent. God is all. God actually transcends our limited view of genders.

My conclusion: I like to think of the Holy Spirit as feminine. In the languages of the Old Testament, Hebrew and Aramaic, the pronoun used for the Spirit is feminine. Another interesting concept is recorded in Genesis in which the plural pronoun is used in the verse about creating man and woman in *our* image (male and female). *Wisdom* is also labeled as *she*, and as noted earlier, *she* was involved in Creation. I believe *Wisdom* and the Holy Spirit are one and the same.

I have also read the books *Finding Holy Spirit Mother* by Ally Kateusz and *Our Mother: The Holy Spirit* by Marianne Widmalm, and their research and views are fascinating. Deidre Havrelock also has interesting information on the topic as does Rev. Salvatore Sapienza in the podcast, "Holy Spirit: Feminine Aspect of God" put forth by Messages from Douglas UCC, dated May 22, 2016. Numerous other conflicting sources are out there for you to do your own research.

Now, please consider the topic.

My sister rolled her eyes at the thought. A friend gave me the "What are you talking about?" look. My daughters and I were able to actually have thoughtful conversations about the topic as we contemplated the idea of a feminine Holy Spirit.

Does it matter?——Does it matter to *you*?

Spiritual Sync routine:

Step One: Spend 10 minutes quieting our world and our hearts before we continue. Today we might use this time to reflect on who the Holy Spirit is based upon our own readings and experience.

Step Two: Scripture—As we begin our 2nd week, we will look at the Holy Spirit in relation to Jesus.

Isaiah 11:1-3a

"A shoot will come up from the stump of Jesse; from his roots a Branch will bear fruit.

The Spirit of the Lord will rest on him—the Spirit of wisdom and of understanding,

the Spirit of counsel and of might, the Spirit of the knowledge and fear of the Lord—

and he will delight in the fear of the Lord."

Luke 1:34-35

"How will this be," Mary asked the angel, 'since I am a virgin?'

The angel answered, 'The Holy Spirit will come on you, and the power of the Most High will overshadow you. So the holy one to be born will be called the Son of God.'"

**I love reading this verse with the idea of a feminine Holy Spirit. Jesus is the Son of God the Father and the Holy Spirit Mother.

The Holy Parents idea can further be defended in the accounts of Jesus' baptism:

Luke 3:21-22

"When all the people were being baptized, Jesus was baptized too. And as he was praying, heaven was opened and the Holy Spirit descended on him in bodily form like a dove. And a voice came from heaven: 'You are my Son, whom I love; with you I am well pleased.'"

Matthew 3:16-17

"As soon as Jesus was baptized, he went up out of the water. At that moment heaven was opened, and he saw the Spirit of God descending like a dove and alighting on him. And a voice from heaven said, 'This is my Son, whom I love; with him I am well pleased.'"

Notice the *and* in both accounts. There is the dove AND there is the voice from heaven. As a mom, I love the idea of both the Heavenly Father and the Holy Spirit being present at the Son's baptism.

Step Three: Pray, reflect, and watch for the Spirit's work in our own lives. What is the Holy Spirit of God saying to us today?

**Please, make your own decision. This is the ideal time to discuss the importance of having our *own personal relationship* with God.

Be determined to regularly ask, "What do I believe?"

Does it matter which pronoun is used? Do we have to agree on this?

We each need to open our hearts and our Scriptures before the Lord during our quiet time and ask God for wisdom and understanding in growing our faith. We will be guided by the wisdom of the Holy Spirit in growing our faith.

Lord God, we believe that You are the Almighty God. We want to know You. We want to have a personal relationship with You. Reveal Yourself to us. In the Name of Jesus Christ. Amen.

"Since we live by the Spirit, let us keep in step with the Spirit." ~*Galatians 5:25*

Day #9 Following the GPS

What did we do in the days before GPS? As if to test this theory a couple of years ago my husband got out the old TomTom as we headed on a long trip. Smartphones in hand, and GoogleMaps at the ready, the rest of the family doubted the logic of perching the gadget on the dash and adjusting the cords along the beverage tray. We even pointed out that we hadn't used the gadget in years. Kevin was not to be deterred. We owned the gadget and we were using it.

Okay. We shared knowing looks, chuckled, and someone said, "Great, let's follow what Grampa TomTom says."

You can all predict how this went. Miles down the road, when "Grampa Tomtom" was confused. We pulled out our updated navigational systems as Kevin sheepishly stuffed the TomTom under his seat.

It wasn't all the TomTom's fault; we hadn't synced the system for years, and obviously, some changes had been made.

The Spiritual Sync is all about staying in sync with God. Jesus knew, even from a young age, that he needed to stay in sync with God. Jesus lived in step with the Spirit throughout his entire life.

What would Jesus do?—He would stay in step with the Spirit.

Spiritual Sync routine:

Step One: We are switching to focus on a different verse, but this one also emphasizes our need to *be still.* **Exodus 14:14** *"The Lord will fight for you; you need only to be still."* Let's take time to be still before the Lord God.

Step Two:

Luke 2:52

"And Jesus grew in wisdom and stature, and in favor with God and man."

*I put the end of the story first, because this is such a wonderful verse to pass on to young people. A goal in life: grow in wisdom and in stature and in favor with God first and also with man.

The rest of the story: Jesus and his family had traveled to Jerusalem and on the return trip Joseph and Mary realized Jesus wasn't with them. They returned to Jerusalem to find him listening and talking with teachers in the temple.

Luke 2:47-49

"Everyone who heard him was amazed at his understanding and his answers. When his parents saw him, they were astonished. His mother said to him, 'Son, why have you treated us like this? Your father and I have been anxiously searching for you.'

'Why were you searching for me?' he asked. 'Didn't you know I had to be in my Father's house?'"

Luke 5:16

"But Jesus often withdrew to lonely places and prayed."

Step Three: Pray, reflect, and watch for the Spirit's work in our own lives. What is the Holy Spirit of God saying to us today?

What would Jesus do? Jesus would (and did) stay in step—in sync—with God. Jesus would quiet his heart and his mind in order to seek God's Holy Spirit for guidance, support, and love. If Jesus knew he needed a navigational system, shouldn't we acknowledge our need for one as well?

Lord God, You are all that we need. We surrender to Your Will for our lives and seek to be still while You fight for us. Help us to grow in wisdom and in stature and in Your favor, God. In Jesus' Name. Amen.

"Since we live by the Spirit, let us keep in step with the Spirit." ~Galatians 5:25

Day #10 Recharge

Isn't it great how our phones will tell us how much battery life is left? On a recent trip we could plan accordingly in order to be sure to get to a place to charge before the last 2% eked out of our phones. In the busy airport, we were sure to plant ourselves by the charging station during our wait, in an attempt to avoid running down.

All of this jockeying in order to be sure our phones don't give out. What are we doing to be sure our spiritual lives don't give out? That is the whole point of this Spiritual Sync.

I know that with all the opportunities life brings, if I am left to myself, I will not make life-giving choices. I will let my spiritual life go into hibernation for a period so that I can do whatever I want.

Today we are going to again look at the example that Jesus left us. Jesus has grown in wisdom and in stature and in favor with God and man. Jesus has also begun his ministry. We started on this path to spiritual strengthening yesterday with Luke 5:16, "But Jesus often withdrew to lonely places and prayed." Notice that Jesus' "charging station" was lonely—without distractions. A place where Jesus could actually connect with God. We should probably follow that same advice in our busy worlds.

Spiritual Sync routine:

Step One: Let's quiet our hearts and minds and connect with the Holy Spirit. Each day can feel like a fight, and in that case, this verse is so encouraging. **Exodus 14:14** *"The Lord will fight for you; you need only to be still."*

Step Two:

Mark 1:35

"Very early in the morning, while it was still dark, Jesus got up, left the house and went off to a solitary place, where he prayed."

Matthew 7:28-29

"When Jesus had finished saying these things, the crowds were amazed at his teaching, because he taught as one who had authority, and not as their teachers of the law."

Luke 10:21a

"At that time Jesus, full of joy through the Holy Spirit, said, 'I praise you, Father, Lord of heaven and earth...'"

Matthew 14:22-23a

"Immediately Jesus made the disciples get into the boat and go on ahead of him to the other side, while he dismissed the crowd. After he had dismissed them, he went up on a mountainside by himself to pray."

What did Jesus do? Jesus recharged.

What did this recharge include?

Quiet.

Prayer.

What did Jesus gain from this recharge?

Joy. Wisdom. Authority. Guidance.

We all seem to have the same tendency about quiet time as we did about nap time when we were toddlers. We fought a nap; we didn't need rest. We wanted to stay up and be big, and our parents were wisely saying, "You need the rest. You'll—we'll—regret it if you don't get a nap."

We will regret it if we don't take time for the Lord. We will suffer the consequences of not being in step with the Spirit—oftentimes that comes in the form of missed blessings. I know I for one don't want to miss blessings from the Most High, and I don't want you to miss any either.

Step Three: Pray, reflect, and watch for the Spirit's work in our own lives. What is the Holy Spirit of God saying to us today? Let's recharge. Let's be still and know that the Almighty God has control, and we just need to get in sync with His blessings and His plan.

Lord God, Thank You for the numerous blessings in our lives. Help us to be still enough to notice and appreciate all the goodness that we have in our lives. Guide us to time to recharge and listen to the Holy Spirit in our lives. In Jesus' Name. Amen.

"Since we live by the Spirit, let us keep in step with the Spirit." ~Galatians 5:25

Day #11 Temptations

Cheetos. Pringles. Nachos. Brownies. Baked pretzels. Cheesecake. Ohhhh, yummm!

When a temptation, like a bowl of crunchy Cheetos, is put within my reach, it is amazing how hungry I can suddenly be. Not only that, no matter what I had been working on, my mind locked in on thoughts of those Cheetos. Temptations can be obvious or subtle, but they still seem to have somewhat of a magnetic power to draw us closer and closer until we cave and all we are left with is regret and fingers full of orange Cheetos dust.

Syncing with the Spirit can help with this, and we have proof in Scripture. Let's look at how Jesus handled temptations that were far more serious than any food cravings.

Spiritual Sync routine:

Step One: Let's quiet our hearts and minds and connect with the Holy Spirit. Is the 10 minutes going by a little faster? I am finding myself yearning to linger longer with the Lord. Today our verse is extra important; when we face challenges and temptations, we certainly would benefit from Spiritual guidance. **Exodus 14:14** *"The Lord will fight for you; you need only to be still."*

Step Two:

Matthew 4:1

"Then Jesus was led by the Spirit into the wilderness to be tempted by the devil."

Luke 4:1-2

"Jesus, full of the Holy Spirit, left the Jordan and was led by the Spirit into the wilderness, where for forty days he was tempted by the devil. He ate nothing during those days, and at the end of them he was hungry."

Acts 10:37-38

"You know what has happened throughout the province of Judea, beginning in Galilee after the baptism that John preached—how God anointed Jesus of Nazareth with the Holy Spirit and power, and how he went around doing good and healing all who were under the power of the devil, because God was with him."

Jesus had to face the enemy on earth. He did. The timing was such that Jesus faced the devil immediately after his baptism. This was also immediately after the anointing of the Holy Spirit and God's proclamation of Jesus as His Son.

Romans 5:1-5

"Therefore, since we have been justified through faith, we have peace with God through our Lord Jesus Christ, through whom we have gained access by faith into this grace in which we now stand. And we boast in the hope of the glory of God. Not only so, but we also glory in our sufferings, because we know that suffering produces perseverance; perseverance, character; and character, hope. And hope does not put us to shame, because

God's love has been poured out into our hearts through the Holy Spirit, who has been given to us."

I Corinthians 10:13

"No temptation has overtaken you except what is common to mankind. And God is faithful; he will not let you be tempted beyond what you can bear. But when you are tempted, he will also provide a way out so that you can endure it."

Jesus was tempted. Jesus was given power through the Holy Spirit to be able to face the temptations and not give in to them. Instead, Jesus recited Scripture as a means of defeating Satan.

What an amazing example for us. While Scripture breaks the news that we will face trials and temptations in our lives, it also provides four truths:

1. Jesus himself was tempted; we have His example to follow when we face our temptations.
2. Jesus was provided the Holy Spirit; we also have access to the Holy Spirit for facing our challenges.
3. Jesus relied on Scripture when rebuking the devil; Scripture has been provided for us to use in facing the difficulties in front of us.
4. God is watching and will provide a way out; God isn't throwing us into the ring alone and unsupervised. He is faithful and watching.

Step Three: Pray, reflect, and brace for those temptations that we know will come our way. Are we prepared? Do we trust the Holy Spirit and God's Word? If so, we will be able to face those trials with confidence.

Lord God, Thank You for the reminder that trials and temptations are common to man. Thank you for setting us up for success as we face these difficulties. Thank you for arming us with the

Holy Spirit and the Bible in order to be strengthened while facing any challenges that come our way today. In Jesus' Name. Amen.

"Since we live by the Spirit, let us keep in step with the Spirit." ~Galatians 5:25

Day #12 Transfiguration

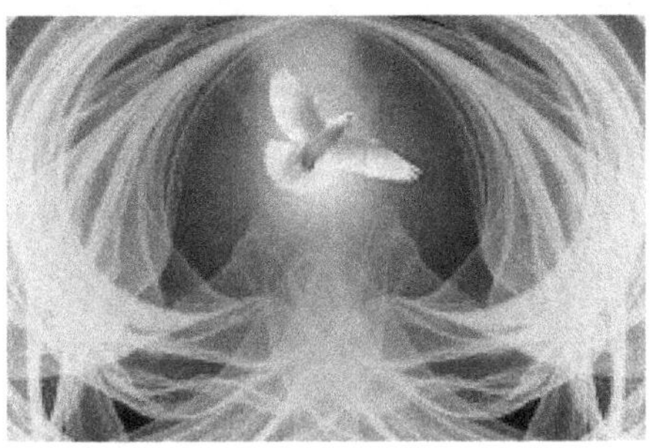

A Homecoming bonfire pep rally can be quite a memorable experience. The crowd gathering, the band playing, the cheerleaders cheering. The energy is electric, and then come the inspiring speeches.

Pep talks are those short speeches packed with powerful analogies and words of wisdom meant to inspire players far beyond the pep rally or the locker room. These motivational moments are meant to carry the warriors onto the battlefield of the game and beyond. (If you need a great read right now, I just finished *The Sender* by Kevin Elko and Bill Beausay; inspiring stories and messages abound in the book.)

Today we are looking at the transfiguration of Jesus; this story is recorded in three of the gospels, and the scene comes days after Jesus has explained to his disciples that he will be dying soon. This is a time when these disciples could certainly use some encouragement.

Spiritual Sync routine:

Step One: 10 minutes of quiet time reflecting on all God has done for us. We can use our verse as a prayer as we begin. *God, Thank you for this day. Please fight for me and teach me to be still. In Jesus' name. Amen.* **Exodus 14:14** *"The Lord will fight for you; you need only to be still."*

Step Two:

Matthew 17: 1-9

"After six days Jesus took with him Peter, James, and John the brother of James, and led them up a high mountain by themselves. There he was transfigured before them. His face shone like the sun, and his clothes became as white as the light. Just then there appeared before them Moses and Elijah, talking with Jesus.

Peter said to Jesus, 'Lord, it is good for us to be here. If you wish, I will put up three shelters—one for you, one for Moses and one for Elijah.'

While he was still speaking, a bright cloud enveloped them, and a voice from the cloud said, 'This is my Son, whom I love; with him I am well pleased. Listen to him!'

When the disciples heard this, they fell face down to the ground, terrified. But Jesus came and touched them, 'Get up,' he said. 'Don't be afraid.' When they looked up, they saw no one except Jesus.

As they were coming down the mountain, Jesus instructed them, 'Don't tell anyone what you have seen, until the Son of Man has been raised from the dead.'"

Observations:

- These three disciples witnessed this powerful visual experience in their alone time with Jesus.

- Peter didn't want this time to end; he wanted to stay and even make shelters!

- God reaffirmed Jesus as the Son of God.

- Jesus told them not to say anything until the time was right.

Step Three: Pray, reflect, and ask what does this mean for each of us?

We looked at this scene from Scripture today because powerful experiences with God also come in our everyday lives.

We need to apply some of those same observations to our own personal experiences with the Lord.

- These events in our lives aren't announced or scheduled. These events will come in God's timing.

- These events will reaffirm us who God is.

- When we have those miraculous moments, we often want to be like Peter and stay there in that miraculous moment. The Holy Spirit will guide us back to our day-to-day living.

- Finally, these times are meant to be shared testimony—when the time is right. We have to trust that just as we were guided to the experience, we will be guided in the sharing of the testimony.

Lord God, Thank You for powerful moments with You. Guide us into the glorious light of Your Word. Help us to be in sync with the Holy Spirit in order to witness Your work in our lives and be willing to share our testimony with others for Your glory, Almighty God. In Jesus' Name. Amen.

"Since we live by the Spirit, let us keep in step with the Spirit." ~Galatians 5:25

Day #13 Submit

Mickey, our Yorkiepoo, is an adorable, stubborn dog. While he may look all cute and cuddly, try getting this willful six pounds on four legs to walk when he doesn't want to go. It isn't pretty. He just resorts to donkey-style stubbornness by digging in those back legs and firmly planting his rear on the ground.

Mickey's defiance kicks in when we head out on a walk and he feels we are leaving someone important behind. Mickey looks at the person in control of the leash, looks at the door, and if not satisfied, firmly plants his rear on the ground and waits as we decide how to best solve the problem.

We all have stubborn tendencies and we all live and work among people who have stubborn tendencies. Obviously, many lessons can be learned about stubbornness.

Today we are looking at how the Holy Spirit can help us let go of our own plans and our own stubbornness in order to submit to God's plan. Specifically, we will look at the example of Jesus submitting to a painful plan with eternal consequences.

Spiritual Sync routine:

Step One: 10 minutes of quiet time reflecting on times we have been stubborn or just breathing slowly and reciting this phrase, "I submit to Your Will for my life, Lord." You can also continue with our verse. **Exodus 14:14,** *"The Lord will fight for you; you need only to be still."* This may be another excellent opportunity for us to go through the Prayer Process from Day #3.

Step Two:

Mark 14:32-36, 41-42 Jesus and his disciples in the Garden of Gethsemane

"They went to a place called Gethsemane, and Jesus said to his disciples, 'Sit here while I pray.' He took Peter, James and John along with him, and he began to be deeply distressed and troubled. 'My soul is overwhelmed with sorrow to the point of death,' he said to them. 'Stay here and keep watch.'

Going a little father, he fell to the ground and prayed that if possible the hour might pass from him. 'Abba, Father,' he said, "everything is possible for you. Take this cup from me. Yet not what I will, but what you will.'

This process is repeated.

"Returning the third time, he said to them, 'Are you still sleeping and resting? Enough! The hour has come. Look, the Son of Man is delivered into the hands of sinners. Rise! Let us go! Here comes my betrayer!'"

Luke 23:46

"Jesus called out with a loud voice, 'Father, into your hands I commit my spirit.' When he had said this, he breathed his last."

*I have abbreviated this to the core act of submission by Jesus, but if time permits, please read each of the Gospel accounts of all that Jesus experienced as he submitted to the will of God the Father.

Step Three: Pray, reflect, and ask what does this mean for each of us in our lives today?

We have all probably experienced a time when someone else had a plan that was different from our own. I'm sure we also have experienced times that the other plan was actually better than our own, and we are glad that we were willing to submit.

We need to follow Jesus' example of bringing our situations to the Lord. Some of the times we will get relief from the pain, and others, as in the case of Jesus, we must go through the hardships. In the long run, God's eternal plan for us is better than anything we can imagine. Today we ask for the Holy Spirit's help in learning to submit each day to what God has planned for us.

Lord God, Thank You for Jesus. Thank you for the example that we see in Jesus' prayer, "Not my will but Thine be done." Help us to continually learn to humbly submit our stubbornness and our will to Your Good and Perfect Plan. In Jesus' Name. Amen.

"Since we live by the Spirit, let us keep in step with the Spirit." ~Galatians 5:25

Day #14 Promises

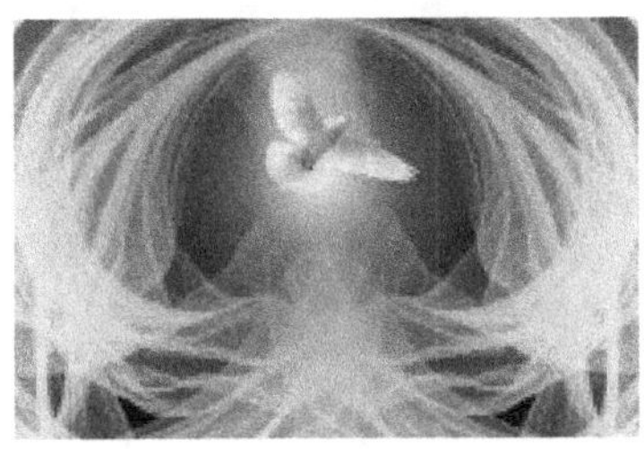

Whenever the Last Supper is mentioned, most of us imagine the mural by Leonardo da Vinci. We picture the table with Jesus at the center and the facial expressions of his followers.

During the Last Supper, Jesus provided the disciples with much more than just food and companionship. John 14 includes three precious promises that Jesus offered to the disciples and to those who trust in him and accept him as their Lord and Savior. Jesus knows that armed with these promises, the disciples would be able to work to fulfill the command that he gives them just before he ascends into heaven.

Spiritual Sync routine:

Step One: 10 minutes of quiet time. **Psalm 46:10,** *"He [God] says, 'Be still, and know that I am God; I will be exalted among the nations, I will be exalted in the earth.'"* Reflect on the sacrifice Jesus made for us.

Step Two: Read all of Chapter 14 if time permits because this is just a glimpse into the words—the messages—that were shared during the Last Supper. These are the precious promises.

Promise #1~A Heavenly Home—-**John 14: 2-3**

"My Father's house has many rooms; if that were not so, would I have told you that I am going to prepare a place for you? And if I go and prepare a place for you, I will come back and take you to be with me that you also may be where I am."

Promise #2~A Holy Guide—-**John 14:25-26**

"'All this I have spoken while still with you. But the Advocate, the Holy Spirit, whom the Father will send in my name, will teach you all things and will remind you of everything I have said to you."

This same promise is later repeated in **Acts 1:8**: *"But you will receive power when the Holy Spirit comes on you; and you will be my witnesses in Jerusalem, and in all Judea and Samaria, and to the ends of the earth."*

Promise #3~A Spiritual Peace—-**John 14:27**

"Peace I leave with you; my peace I give to you. I do not give to you as the world gives. Do not let your hearts be troubled and do not be afraid."

The Command~**Matthew 28:18-20**

"Then Jesus came to them and said, 'All authority in heaven and on earth has been given to me. Therefore go and make disciples of all nations, baptizing them in the name of the Father and of the Son and of the Holy Spirit, and teaching them to obey everything I have commanded you. And surely I am with you always, to the very end of the age.'"

Step Three: Pray, reflect, and ask the Holy Spirit to guide us in a response.

An eternal home, a Spiritual Guide, and peace! What a reward from the Lord! Let's use our gifts wisely as we serve the Lord to help fulfill His Command.

Lord God, How remarkable! Not only did Jesus offer the ultimate sacrifice, but in addition, You bless us with peace, the Holy Spirit, and heaven. Lord, we are humbled by Your generosity. Guide

us in using these gifts well as the Spirit leads us. In Jesus' Name. Amen.

"Since we live by the Spirit, let us keep in step with the Spirit." ~Galatians 5:25

Day #15 Pouring

When a storm is brewing outside, in true Nebraska fashion, many onlookers take to their porches or decks to watch the action. We are awaiting the gusts of winds and the downpour that may or may not come from the billowing clouds above us.

I certainly have been guilty of seeking the action of the storm rather than seeking shelter from the storm. I have never gone so far as to be a storm chaser, but those folks do what they do to observe storms and learn more about them. Where best to gain this insight than to be up close to the wind and the fury?

The disciples have endured the tumultuous time of Jesus' arrest, crucifixion, and burial. They have experienced the empty tomb and the miraculous visits from their Lord and Savior.

Today we get the exciting look at the action when Jesus' promises at the Last Supper are fulfilled! The "storm" of Pentecost is filled with strong winds and tongues of fire. The outpouring of the Holy Spirit certainly doesn't go unnoticed.

Spiritual Sync routine:

Step One: 10 minutes of quiet time reflecting on God's promises. I would highly encourage some Christian music in the background. "Alexa, play K-Love radio." or "Alexa, play My Bridge radio."

Step Two: Imagine you are a movie director with modern technology, and you are about to film this scene. Read the passage and try to visualize how you would create this scene for the big screen.

Acts 2:1-12, 14, & 32-33 I separated the verses at first just to help us create the magnificence of the scene. This is also abridged; if time allows, please read all of Acts 2.

"When the day of Pentecost came, they were all together in one place.

Suddenly a sound like the blowing of a violent wind came from heaven and filled the whole house where they were sitting.

They saw what seemed to be tongues of fire that separated and came to rest on each of them.

All of them were filled with the Holy Spirit and began to speak in other tongues as the Spirit enabled them.

Now there were staying in Jerusalem God-fearing Jews from every nation under heaven.

When they heard this sound, a crowd came together in bewilderment, because each one heard their own language being spoken.

Utterly amazed, they asked: 'Aren't all these who are speaking Galileans? Then how is it that each of us hears them in our native language? ...—we hear them declaring the wonders of God in our own tongues!'

Amazed and perplexed, they asked one another, 'What does this mean?'

Then Peter stood up with the Eleven, raised his voice and addressed the crowd: 'Fellow Jews and all of you who live in Jerusalem, let me explain this to you; listen carefully to what I say...God has raised this Jesus to life, and we are all witnesses of it. Exalted to the right hand of God, he has received from the Father the promised Holy Spirit and has poured out what you now see and hear.'"

Acts 4:31

"After they prayed, the place where they were meeting was shaken. And they were all filled with the Holy Spirit and spoke the word of God boldly."

Step Three: Pray, reflect, and ask what does this magnificent scene mean for each of us?

We realize that God's Spirit can be a still, small voice, and God's Spirit can be a mighty gust. However, it still amazes me that God's Spirit lives in you and in me and in all believers. The Spirit wants to be active in our lives. Let it sink in that God wants to bring this type of scene to life in us—one in which we act and speak in sync with the Holy Spirit. Let us welcome the outpouring of the Holy Spirit in our own lives.

After all, we know that the gift of the Holy Spirit is a gift from our Maker—our Heavenly Father. A lot of us are able to understand the gift-giving mentality of a parent, and **Luke 11:13** states the thought very well, *"If you then, though you are evil, know how to give good gifts to your children, how much more will your Father in heaven give the Holy Spirit to those who ask him!"* Let's be willing to be bold and ask God to pour the Holy Spirit into each of our lives.

Lord God, Thank You for the gift of your Holy Spirit; we boldly ask that You pour the Holy Spirit into our hearts. Help us to feel the stirring of the Spirit in our hearts and submit to Your Will. Guide us this day and open our eyes, ears, hearts, and minds to the action of the Spirit. In Jesus' Name. Amen.

"Since we live by the Spirit, let us keep in step with the Spirit." ~Galatians 5:25

Day #16 Impact

"An impact is the measure of an action's benefit to society and the planet," according to Sir Ronald Cohen in his book *On Impact: The Guide to the Impact Revolution*. Merriam-Webster defines *impact* as "the force of impression of one thing on another."

So what was the impact of the gift of the Holy Spirit at Pentecost? The scene was impressive, but did it create a forceful impression on the people who witnessed it? Did it meet Cohen's definition? Do we have the ability to "measure the action's benefit to society and the planet"?

In order to find out, we need to read the end of Acts 2 *and* while we do that, we need to also consider whether we are letting these words sink into our own hearts and minds. We will know our Spiritual Sync is successful if we are willing to allow the Spirit to make an impression in our own lives.

Spiritual Sync routine:

Step One: 10 minutes of quiet time reflecting on God's promises. Today we might begin with imagining our scene from yesterday and thanking God for the amazing gift of the Spirit as we also tell ourselves to "Be still."

Step Two: Here is the rest of the story of Pentecost...

Acts 2:37-42

"When the people heard this, they were cut to the heart and said to Peter and the other apostles, 'Brothers, what shall we do?'

Peter replied, 'Repent and be baptized, every one of you, in the name of Jesus Christ for the forgiveness of your sins. And you will receive the gift of the Holy Spirit. The promise is for you and your children and for all who are far off—for all whom the Lord our God will call.'

With many other words he warned them; and he pleaded with them, 'Save yourselves from this corrupt generation.'

<u>Those who accepted his message were baptized, and about three thousand were added to their number that day.</u>"

Three thousand.

3,000!

They saw. They listened. They believed.

Then...

They repented, were baptized, and received the gift of the Holy Spirit.

Jesus promised the gift, he submitted to God's Will, he suffered and died and rose again. Those actions have left an immeasurable impact in this world and in eternity.

Now hopefully our hearts are open to what we have seen, and we too, are asking, "What shall we do?" The answer is still the same. Repent, be baptized, and accept the gift of the Holy Spirit.

Step Three: Pray, reflect, and ask what does this mean for each of us? It is time for each of us to get personal with God and have a heart-to-heart talk. We each might say the following:

Lord God, I thank You for the impact of Your Son and Your Spirit. I ask for your forgiveness. I am a sinner in need of a Savior. I believe Jesus Christ is that Savior. I submit to Your Will for my life. Fill me with Your Holy Spirit, Lord, that I may serve you. In Jesus' Name. Amen.

"Since we live by the Spirit, let us keep in step with the Spirit." ~Galatians 5:25

Day #17 Up for a Challenge?

I decided to put a challenge to myself this week: my own mini-version of a triathlon. I made the decision to do it the day before, so I did have a plan in mind. I started the morning with a 3.1 mile run, I swam for a mile at lunch, and then rode my bike 3 miles in the evening.

I'm certainly not ready for the Olympics or anything, but I have to say I was fired up about the challenge. I did have some fear as to whether I could accomplish the tasks, and I had even more concerns about the aches and pains I would have as a result.

This athletic challenge was nothing compared to some of life's real challenges that we encounter in our day-to-day lives: abuse, illness, grief, addiction, death, etc.

A challenge is also put before us when the Holy Spirit is given. That challenge is to listen to the Holy Spirit. To use the Holy Spirit. To let the Holy Spirit guide us on the comfortable, relaxing shore line and even into the deep, turbulent waters in order to build our faith and to strengthen us in order to allow us to be witnesses to others.

Spiritual Sync routine:

Step One: If possible, listen to "Oceans" ("Where Feet May Fail") by Hillsong United. Meditate on the state of our faith. Are we prepared for a challenge from the Holy Spirit?

Step Two: Scripture Let's explore several verses that attest to the various challenges we may be asked to face as believers.

John 15:26-27

"When the Advocate comes, whom I will send to you from the Father—the Spirit of truth who goes out from the Father—he will testify about me. And you also must testify, for you have been with me from the beginning."

I John 4:13-15

"This is how we know that we live in him and he in us: He has given us of his Spirit. And we have seen and testify that the Father has sent his Son to be the Savior of the world. If anyone acknowledges that Jesus is the Son of God, God lives in them and they in God."

Romans 5:3-5

"Not only so, but we also glory in our sufferings, because we know that suffering produces perseverance; perseverance, character; and character, hope. And hope does not put us to shame, because God's love has been poured out into our hearts through the Holy Spirit, who has been given to us."

Mark 13:11

"Whenever you are arrested and brought to trial, do not worry beforehand about what to say. Just say whatever is given you at the time, for it is not you speaking, but the Holy Spirit."

Acts 6:8-10

"Now Stephen, a man full of God's grace and power, performed great wonders and signs among the people. Opposition arose, however, from members of the Synagogue...but they could not stand up against the wisdom the Spirit gave him as he spoke."

Acts 7:54-58a

"When the members of the Sanhedrin heard this, they were furious and gnashed their teeth at him. But Stephen, full of the Holy Spirit, looked up to heaven and saw the glory of God, and Jesus standing at the right hand of God. 'Look,' he said, 'I see heaven open and the Son of Man standing at the right hand of God.'

At this they covered their ears and, yelling at the top of their voices, they all rushed at him, dragged him out of the city and began to stone him."

Acts 7:55

"But Stephen, full of the Holy Spirit, looked up to heaven and saw the glory of God, and Jesus standing at the right hand of God."

Step Three: Pray, reflect, and ask what does this mean for us? Again, we need to get personal with God now and have another heart-to-heart talk. Be aware that each day will come with challenges. Some of those challenges will be minor inconveniences, others may overwhelm us entirely. God's Spirit will be there for us whatever the struggle.

Lord God, thank You for the Holy Spirit. Thank you for opportunities in which to serve and to glorify You, Heavenly Father.

Guide us in our daily living and help us to turn to You with each challenge that we face. In Jesus' Name. Amen.

"Since we live by the Spirit, let us keep in step with the Spirit." ~Galatians 5:25

Day #18 Bearing Fruit

Growing up, I enjoyed it when our youth group would sing the Christian song, "They Will Know We are Christians." The song has an upbeat rhythm, and part of the lyrics are as follows:

"We are one in the Spirit, we are one in the Lord

We are one in the Spirit, we are one in the Lord

And we pray that all unity may one day be restored

And they'll know we are Christians by our love, by our love

They will know we are Christians by our love..."

One in the Spirit. One in the Lord. One. United. Not divided.

Today, we often complicate matters far more than we need to, but as the song states, we should be one. More importantly, people should be able to "know we are Christians by our love." Being guided by the Spirit, we should bring forth fruit...the fruit of the Spirit.

Spiritual Sync routine:

Step One: Reflect on our spiritual walks and the "fruit" that has come from it lately. Do we feel as if we have been bringing forth fruit?—Or has our growth been stagnant?

Step Two: We are intended to grow and mature as we read God's Word.

John 15: 1-5

"I am the true vine, and my Father is the gardener. He cuts off every branch in me that bears no fruit, while every branch that does bear fruit he prunes so that it will be even more fruitful. You are already clean because of the word I have spoken to you. Remain in me, as I also remain in you. No branch can bear fruit by itself; it must remain in the vine. Neither can you bear fruit unless you remain in me.

I am the vine; you are the branches. If you remain in me and I in you, you will bear much fruit; apart from me you can do nothing."

Matthew 7:16-18

"By their fruit you will recognize them. Do people pick grapes from thornbushes, or figs from thistles? Likewise, every good tree bears good fruit, but a bad tree bears bad fruit. A good tree cannot bear bad fruit, and a bad tree cannot bear good fruit."

Galatians 5:22-23

"But the fruit of the Spirit is love, joy, peace, forbearance, kindness, goodness, faithfulness, gentleness, and self-control. Against such things there is no law."

Romans 15:5-6, & 13

"May the God who gives endurance and encouragement give you the same attitude of mind toward each other that Christ Jesus had, so that with one mind and one voice you may glorify the God and Father of our Lord Jesus Christ."

"May the God of hope fill you with all joy and peace as you trust in him, so that you may overflow with hope by the power of the Holy Spirit."

2 Corinthians 3:3 & 16-18

"You show that you are a letter from Christ, the result of our ministry, written not with ink but with the Spirit of the living God, not on tablets of stone but on tablets of human hearts."

"But whenever anyone turns to the Lord, the veil is taken away. Now the Lord is the Spirit, and where the Spirit of the Lord is, there is freedom. And we all, who with unveiled faces contemplate the Lord's glory, are being transformed into his image with ever-increasing glory, which comes from the Lord, who is the Spirit."

Step Three: Pray, reflect, and ask what does this mean for each of us? What fruit are each of us producing? Do we each need to be open to some "pruning" in our lives?

Almighty God, We thank you for seasons of growth. We even thank you for the pruning that You do in our lives. Help us to continue to grow stronger and more mature in our faith. Help us to respond to the guidance of the Holy Spirit and to bear much fruit. May we give you the glory and may others be able to truly know we are Christians by our love. In Jesus' Name. Amen.

"Since we live by the Spirit, let us keep in step with the Spirit." ~Galatians 5:25

Day #19 Valuable Lesson

I asked for it, and I learned a valuable lesson. This weekend Kevin & I ran in a 5K. Beforehand, I asked him to set the pace, because I tend to start too slow. So, he did just what I asked, and set the pace...and I was sucking air the entire 3+ miles...I survived, and as I already stated, learned a valuable lesson.

The Lesson: I had my own pace—a steady, comfortable pace. Following the pace of someone else was a struggle; it was challenging and difficult. However, the end result was what I wanted—a faster time.

The Spiritual Lesson: I have my own plan for my day; I wake up with to-do lists floating through my head. Following the plan of the Holy

Spirit may be a struggle; it will at times be challenging and difficult. However, the end result will be what I want and need—a life lived for Christ.

Spiritual Sync routine:

Step One: 10 minutes of quiet time clearing our minds of our own plans and to-do lists for the day. Take a deep breath and say aloud, "I surrender my own plans today." This may be another great opportunity to follow the Prayer Process from Day #3.

Step Two: God's Spirit has a course and a pace set out for us each and every day.

I Corinthians 9:24-27

"Do you not know that in a race all the runners run, but only one gets the prize? Run in such a way as to get the prize. Everyone who competes in the games goes into strict training. They do it to get a crown that will not last, but we do it to get a crown that will last forever. Therefore I do not run like someone running aimlessly; I do not fight like a boxer beating the air. No, I strike a blow to my body and make it my slave so that after I have preached to others, I myself will not be disqualified for the prize."

Hebrews 12:1-3

"Therefore, since we are surrounded by such a great cloud of witnesses, let us throw off everything that hinders and the sin that so easily entangles. And let us run with perseverance the race marked out for us, fixing our eyes on Jesus, the pioneer and perfecter of faith. For the joy set before him he endured the cross, scorning its shame, and sat down at the right hand of the

throne of God. Consider him who endured such opposition from sinners, so that you will not grow weary and lose heart."

Isaiah 40:28-31

"Do you not know? Have you not heard? The Lord is the everlasting God, the Creator of the ends of the earth.

He will not grow tired or weary, and his understanding no one can fathom.

He gives strength to the weary and increases the power of the weak.

Even youths grow tired and weary, and young men stumble and fall;

but those who hope in the Lord will renew their strength.

They will soar on wings like eagles;

they will run and not grow weary,

they will walk and not be faint."

2 Timothy 4:7

"I have fought the good fight, I have finished the race, I have kept the faith. Now there is in store for me the crown of righteousness, which the Lord, the righteous Judge, will award to me on that day—and not only to me, but also to all who have longed for his appearing."

Step Three: Pray, reflect, and ask what does this mean for me?

This valuable lesson is worth it. Learn to run this race of life in sync with the Holy Spirit. *It's worth it!*

Heavenly Father, You are great and mighty, Lord, and we trust in You and in Your plan for our lives. Help us today to submit to the

Holy Spirit. Let us not grow weary in doing Your Will. Guide us in growing in our faith. In Jesus' Name. Amen.

"Since we live by the Spirit, let us keep in step with the Spirit." ~Galatians 5:25

Day #20 In Your Corner

I know very little about boxing and, honestly, have a difficult time watching a bout without shielding my eyes from the blood of the battle. My husband's father was a champion boxer in his day. He obviously knew the ins and outs of the struggle in the ring, and he definitely understood the power of having someone in his corner.

Martin C. Baldridge

We are nearing the end of our 21-Day Sync with the Spirit, and today we are looking at how the Holy Spirit is "in our corner" just like a prize fighter has someone in his/her corner.

Summer Sync routine:

    Step One: 10 minutes—Today, let's go ahead and take a few of those moments to think through our schedules for the day. Let's submit to the

Holy Spirit's guiding over some of those tasks on our to-do lists, and also give thanks that the Holy Spirit is "in our corner" through all of what we will encounter today.

Step Two: Each and every day the Spirit is busy on our behalf. *As we read these verses today, let's imagine a boxing match going on and that these are words we are hearing from our corner.*

Round One Bell—-**Ephesians 1: 17**

"I keep asking that the God of our Lord Jesus Christ, the glorious Father, may give you the Spirit of wisdom and revelation, so that you may know him better."

...We're feeling pretty good.

Round Two Bell—-**Romans 8:26-27**

"In the same way, the Spirit helps us in our weakness. We do not know what we ought to pray for, but the Spirit himself intercedes for us through wordless groans. And he who searches our hearts knows the mind of the Spirit, because the Spirit intercedes for God's people in accordance with the will of God."

...We got pretty beat up during that round, but we were resolute to keep battling.

Round Three Bell—-**Romans 8:14 & 16**

"For those who are led by the Spirit of God are the children of God."

"The Spirit himself testifies with our spirit that we are God's children."

...We felt unusually strong during the battle. We threw some strong punches and the enemy staggered a little.

Round Four Bell—-**Romans 8:38-39**

"For I am convinced that neither death nor life, neither angels nor demons, neither the present nor the future, nor any powers, neither height nor depth, nor anything else in all creation, will be able to separate us from the love of God that is in Christ Jesus our Lord."

...We've got the enemy on the ropes. He wanted to throw in the towel and was just saved by the bell. We are worn but energized; we are not sure where the energy is coming from, but we feel light on our feet and supported.

Round Five—-**Ephesians 3:20-21**

"Now to him who is able to do immeasurably more than all we ask or imagine, according to his power that is at work within us, to him be glory in the church and in Christ Jesus throughout all generations, for ever and ever! Amen."

...IT'S A KNOCKOUT!!!! *Those words from our corner guided us to a fabulous finish!*

The Aftermath—-**Romans 8:18**

"I consider that our present sufferings are not worth comparing with the glory that will be revealed in us."

Step Three: Pray, reflect, and ask what does this mean for each of us?

Life is so much more than a boxing match, but at the core it is a battle and we have the benefit of already knowing that God wins. We definitely want to be in the winner's corner. Today, let's be willing to go in the ring for the Lord witnessing all He has done in our lives.

Lord God, each day as we enter the ring to face our challenges, we want the Holy Spirit in the ring with us. Help us to hear and experience the encouragement that the Spirit offers us throughout our challenges. Thank you, God. In Jesus' Name. Amen.

"Since we live by the Spirit, let us keep in step with the Spirit."~Galatians 5:25

Day #21 Fan into Flames

Summertime means relaxing in front of a cozy campfire and cooking s'mores, right?

a cozy campfire

my husband's version

On this our last day of our Spiritual Sync: 21 Days of Syncing with the Spirit, we are not going to be focusing on being comfortable in front of a small, cozy fire. We are trying to ignite the kind of campfire my husband likes to tend—or better yet, the type of pep rally bonfire that an entire community can unite around while singing the school song.

Before we get to that, let's review yesterday's focus: the Holy Spirit being "in our corner." Two important reminders for our day-to-day fight:

1. **Ephesians 6:10-13,** *"Finally, be strong in the Lord and in his mighty power. Put on the full armor of God, so that you can take your stand against the devil's schemes. For our struggle is not against flesh and blood, but against the rulers, against the authorities, against the powers of this dark world and against the spiritual forces of evil in the heavenly realms."* If time permits, continue reading the rest of Ephesians 6 in order to read about each element of the armor that God provides us for this day-to-day spiritual fight.

2. **Exodus 14:14,** *"The Lord will fight for you; you need only to be still."* We are all facing various difficult battles right now, and I just want to reassure everyone that some battles were meant to be fought in our corner of the ring on our knees instead of face-to-face with the enemy. We aren't throwing in the towel; we are letting our Maker battle for us as is promised in this scripture. **Ephesians 6:18**, *"And pray in the Spirit on all occasions with all kinds of prayers and requests. With this in mind, be alert and always keep on praying for all the Lord's people."*

3. **Ezekiel 36:26-27,** *"I will give you a new heart and put a new spirit in you; I will remove from you your heart of stone and give you a heart of flesh. And I will put my Spirit in you and move you to follow my decrees and be careful to keep my law."* <u>This fight can and will harden our hearts if we let it! God, of course, knows this, and that is why this promise is given in the Bible</u>. It's okay, offer your hardened heart back to God and let the Spirit fill you with a tender heart of flesh. Life is so much more beautiful this way! Trust me, I've done it.

Spiritual Sync routine:

Step One: Let's quiet our hearts. We might begin with thanking God for meeting us wherever we are. I recommend closing your eyes and listening to the message in the song "Pass It On"[1]

Step Two: Back to Fanning into Flame...

2 Timothy 1:6-7

"For this reason I remind you to fan into flame the gift of God, which is in you through the laying on of my hands. For the Spirit God gave us does not make us timid, but gives us power, love and self-discipline."

Fan into flames—We have some work to do. Getting a fire going can be tricky. It does take time and effort. We may have a spark one moment and it disappears the next. With time and effort, we can build a fire.

One light, one sparkler is wonderful, but a group of sparklers is captivating, it's mesmerizing, and it certainly makes more of an impact.

---

1.   https://www.blogger.com/blog/post/edit/307257014336804810/2924760311792635722#

...fan into flame the gift of God...

We now know that the gift of God isn't fame, glory, or money. The gift is much more powerful, valuable, and consistent than any of these.

The gift is the Holy Spirit of the Most High God.

From Creation, throughout the miracles of the Old and New Testaments, through the life, death and resurrection of Jesus, to the great gust of wind and the flames at Pentecost, to our hearts today, the Spirit of God gives power, love, and self-discipline.

Now that we realize what this gift that we have received is and are aware of the fruit that comes from this gift, <u>let us indeed, fan into flames this gift of God!</u>

Ecclesiastes 3:11

"He has made everything beautiful in its time. He has also set eternity in the human heart; yet no one can fathom what God has done from beginning to end."

***Isn't that *beautiful*? *"...He has also set eternity in the human heart..."* The Holy Spirit was there at Creation, is here in our hearts now, and has even brought the view of heaven into our hearts as well. We can trust that our current place on this earth is not our eternal home.

Step Three: Pray, reflect, and ask what does this mean for each of us today?

God's Spirit can be a still, small voice, and God's Spirit can be a mighty gust. God's Spirit lives in you and in me and in all believers. The Spirit wants to be more than a small flicker in our lives. God wants the light in each of us to build, and that is why we must fan into flames this gift of the Spirit.

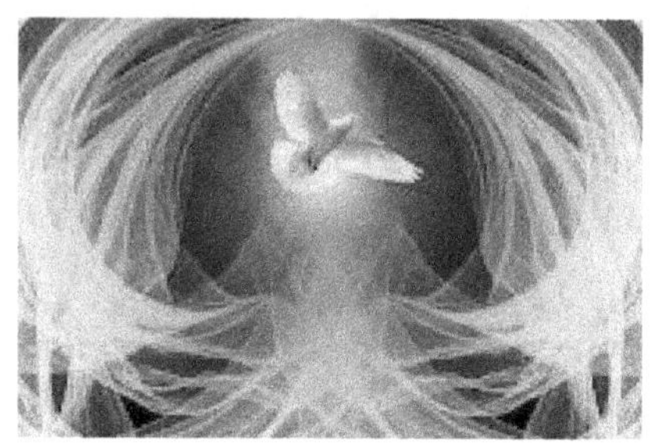

Lord God, Thank You for this time to get to know You and the Holy Spirit better. Help us to take time each day to be still in order to feel the stirring of the Spirit in our hearts and submit to Your Will. Guide us this day and open our eyes, ears, hearts, and minds to the action of the Spirit and let us truly fan into flames Your magnificent Holy Spirit. In Jesus' Name. Amen.

"Since we live by the Spirit, let us keep in step with the Spirit." ~Galatians 5:25

Sync Successful!

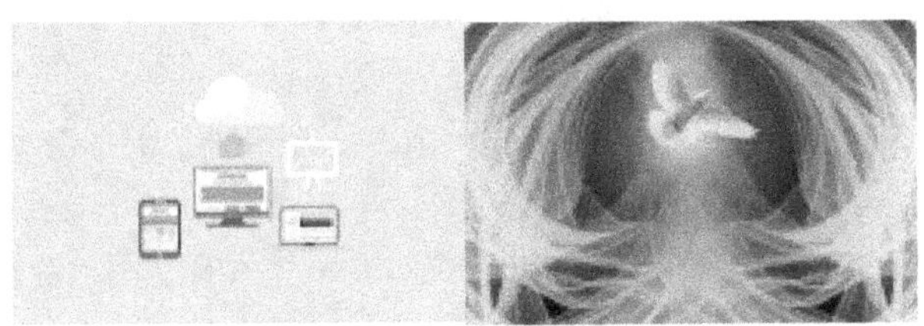

Congratulations! We have reached the end of our 21-Day Sync with the Spirit! I hope it was as rewarding for you as it was for me. Remember, my own spirit needed some extra time to sync with the Holy Spirit, and I felt led to encourage someone else to join me on the journey.

Feel free to revisit any of the pages at any time, and encourage others to grow spiritually by encouraging them to also sync with the Holy Spirit.

Our purpose from the start:

- Our technology needs time to sync.

● It stands to reason that our spiritual lives also need time to sync.

We wanted to stop, connect, and allow time for us to sync with our Maker—to sync our spirit with God's Holy Spirit.

A few words of encouragement and reminders before we wrap up this Spiritual Sync in prayer.

Psalm 143:8-10 (*Words from David, a man full of the Spirit and a man after God's own heart) A reminder to meet with God each morning and ask for the Spirit to lead us.

"Let the morning bring me word of your unfailing love,
for I have put my trust in you.
Show me the way I should go, for to you I entrust my life.
Rescue me from my enemies, Lord, for I hide myself in you.
Teach me to do your will, for you are my God;
may your good Spirit lead me on level ground."

Psalm 51: 10-11 (*Words from David, when he was begging forgiveness of the Lord) We may want to include these words in our own prayers.

"Create in me a pure heart, O God, and renew a steadfast spirit within me.

Do not cast me from your presence or take your Holy Spirit from me."

I Thessalonians 5:19

"Do not quench the Spirit."

Ephesians 4:29-30

"Do not let any unwholesome talk come out of your mouths, but only what is helpful for building others up according to their needs, that it may benefit those who listen. And do not grieve the Holy Spirit of God, with whom you were sealed for the day of redemption."

I Thessalonians 5: 11

"Therefore encourage one another and build each other up, just as in fact you are doing."

Micah 6:8 *This is so good, I had to repeat it one more time.

"He has shown you, O mortal, what is good. And what does the Lord require of you?

To act justly and to love mercy and to walk humbly with your God."

Okay, seriously, this is the last one...**Isaiah 30:21**

"Whether you turn to the right or to the left, your ears will hear a voice behind you, saying, 'This is the way; walk in it.'" **That voice is the precious voice of the Holy Spirit wanting to lead us on our way.**

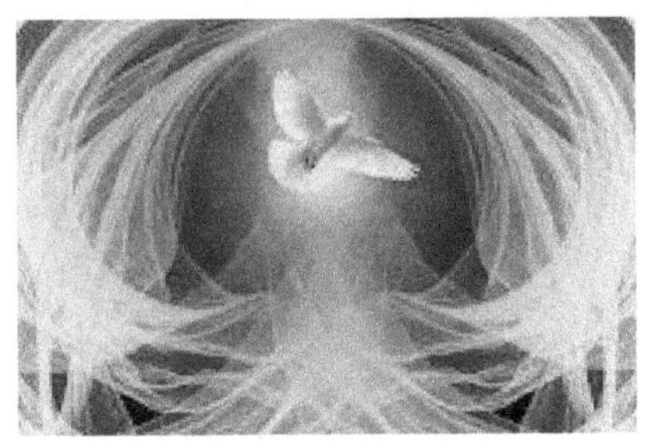

Lord God, Thank you for the Advocate, the gift of the Holy Spirit. Help us to submit to the Spirit and to become more familiar with the Holy Spirit's leading in our lives. Guide us to grow in our faith and to know Your Holy Word, Lord. Let us go on from here to encourage others to sync with the Spirit. In Jesus' Name. Amen.

"Since we live by the Spirit, let us keep in step with the Spirit." ~Galatians 5:25

Notes

The Scripture references in this work are from the *New International Version* unless otherwise noted.

Much of this work was first published on one of my blogs entitled, "The Summer Sync: 21 Days of Syncing with the Spirit." The entries were posted in June of 2021.

I need to send a thank you to my family for their love, smiles, support, and encouragement. Thanks also to Audrey for her critiques and support.

As always, I look back on a project and am in amazement that I am standing at a finish line. It is then that I close my eyes (yes, as tears well up) take a deep breath and thank God for His unending patience with me.

Hebrews 12:1-2a

"Therefore, since we are surrounded by such a great cloud of witnesses, let us throw off everything that hinders and the sin that so easily entangles. And let us run with perseverance the race marked out for us, fixing our eyes on Jesus, the pioneer and perfecter of faith..."

www.ingramcontent.com/pod-product-compliance
Lightning Source LLC
Chambersburg PA
CBHW071354130726
47996CB00002B/930